LIFE CANNOT LIVE
WITHOUT DEATH
&
DEATH CANNOT LIVE
WITHOUT LIFE

Books by Ayin M. Adams

For the Love of Black Men

Good Orderly Direction

For Ladies Only, Dedicated to the Color Pink

Kwanzaa in Hawai`i

African Americans In Hawai`i: A Search For Identity

The Woods Deep Inside Me

Walking In Sappho's Garden

Walking Through My Fire

Books edited by Ayin M. Adams

Climbing A Rainbow of Dreams

Butterflies Blossom

From Dawn To Dusk

Graffiti Dreams

LIFE CANNOT LIVE WITHOUT DEATH
&
DEATH CANNOT LIVE WITHOUT LIFE

Ayin M. Adams, Msc.D., Ph.D.

DELANE PUBLISHING

Copyright © 2016 by Ayin M. Adams

ISBN 13
978-0-9906139-9-2

First Edition: November 2016

Author's Photo by Ayin M. Adams
Cover Design and Typesetting by Saforabu Graphix
Cross In The Heaven Photo courtesy of Monika Wisniewska | Dreamstime.com
Nazareth Village Replica Tomb Photo courtesy of S Comer
Back Cover Design: Trinity Knot symbol, represents life, death, rebirth, Father, Son, and Holy Spirit. Its three equal arcs represent equality, its continuous line expresses eternity, and the interweaving represents indivisibility and unity.

Published by Delane Publishing
P.O. Box 195, Wailuku, Maui, HI 96793 USA
Email: books@delanepublishing.com
www.delanepublishing.com

Published in the United States of America

No part of this book may be reproduced or transmitted in any form or by any means, electronic, photocopying, or otherwise, without the express written consent of the publisher.

Printed in USA

Dedication

To the ever unfolding, releasing, expression of love and the gift of life within you. Receive it and embrace it.

Contents

Preface	viii
Acknowledgements	x
Introduction	xi
Section I - Life Cannot Live Without Death	**1**
The Eternal Secret of Life	2
Nothing Echoes	3
Life after Death	4
Life- Death Cycles	5
Prayer	6
Speak to Me	7
Death Decaying	8
When At Last We Can No Longer Breathe	10
Belonging By Birth	12
Life Cannot Live Without Death & Death Cannot Live Without Life	13
Section II - Death Cannot Live Without Life	**15**
A White Stone	16
Life after Death	18
Restless Shadows	20
The Gap	22
Cease Clinging to Me	24
Alone	25
Who Is Responsible For You	26
Even After Death	28
Hellos and Goodbyes	30
Mystery	31
Life is Temporal	32
Section III - The Continuity of Life	**33**
Dear Mother,	34
Spiritual Mind Treatments	37
Steps for Giving a Spiritual Mind Treatment	41
Scriptural Readings	44
The Will of God	48
Imaging Exercise: Prayer	49
About the Author	*51*

Preface

Dr. Ayin Adams is alive with a Spirit that burns with intense passion and courage. It is this fearlessness that is alive in the brilliant radiance of the words shared in "Life Cannot Live Without Death and Death Cannot Live Without Life."

There is the depth of her background that reaches the heights of our soul with compassion that experience can only bring for us to feel and know. She has written eight books and has received an impressive list of awards for her work. But this is just a reflection of the way God works through Dr. Ayin Adams, for she has asked to serve her purpose and her voice has been heard and recognized.

In this new book she speaks to us about the truth of life and death. This is a subject many would back away from. It has been said that fools rush in where angels fear to tread. But Dr. Ayin is not a fool and the angels and God have seen the need for the truth to be shared about death as one of our greatest teachers.

Those who have a higher understanding believe life has no beginning and no ending. This is wisdom we can hold on to when we are face to face with the truth of the dance of life and death. However, when one is facing the reality of death there are so many fears that arise that it is difficult to hold onto anything.

The words shared here are not just words. For it is so hard to express how life and death touch our lives. Just go through any Facebook post about how someone is facing death and see how totally helpless we are to try to reach out to someone who is suffering and in pain. So words if they are just words would fall short of offering the truth of our limited existence here on Earth and how we deal with the loss of a loved one.

The words shared here are more than words. They are Spirit speaking through Dr. Ayin Adams. They are the inspiration and the feeling we want to proclaim and yet always fall short of saying.

You will feel the depth of loss and the triumph of life that survives beyond this physical form.

You will be inspired and you will nod your head in silent agreement.

You will be touched to your soul.

Dr. Ayin Adams has, through her connection to Spirit, called upon the power of God's energy to bring you words you can believe in. For there are words beyond words that you can live with and read over and over again to savor and feed your hungry soul.

So open up the door to your heart and receive the blessings of the love and wisdom that will resonate within as you read this offering given to us by Dr. Ayin Adams. For in truth, "Life cannot live without death and death cannot live without life."

Rev. Dr. Cindy Paulos, author of; *Angel Blessings and Messages from Heaven*

Acknowledging the One Universal God
in which we live, move, and have our being in;
the continuity of life.

Introduction

I want to write about the continuity of life. I want to share with you that death is a pause and then we live again. I want you to know that life cannot live without death and death cannot live without life. You must first understand that death is not a passport to another world; it is a quality of perception for this one. Now is the times to take a new look at ourselves and contemplate the Divine process within us. It is time to reappraise the principle that makes all overcoming possible. There is an eternal secret involved in the resurrection of life after death. It is the same secret involve in nature at springtime, then the metamorphosis of the caterpillar into the butterfly, then the healing of the slightest cut on my finger. Paul once cried out, "oh that I knew him in the power of his resurrection. Paul was speaking about Jesus. You want to know not what just might have happened to Jesus, but what was the eternal message of the resurrection principle, that's what we want to know? I believe that there is a principle involved that we may have overlooked in our studies of the universe around us and our evaluation of the world within us.

Ask the average person in church today, what Easter is all about? They will probably say it commemorates Jesus resurrection from the tomb. Do you know that it has almost nothing to say to the immediate moment? Easter is not just a day on which something happened to Jesus, it is what happened in him, there is an eternal secret involved; a principle and a process that is repeatable. The eternal secret of life after death is that resurrection is a quality of life and there's no completely understanding of life without it.

This is powerfully suggested by the story of a little girl who was crying uncontrollably as she look out the front window of her home watching her brothers dragged the lifeless form of her pet dog that had been run over in the road. She was crushed. Her Quaker grandfather stood by her, put his hand lovingly on her head, comforting her, as the boys buried the dog. The Quaker grandfather took her lovingly by the hand, led her to a side window, looking out into the garden where a little tree she had planted in the fall was in full bloom. Suddenly she began to squeal with sheer delight. The wise man said, "You see dear, you were looking out the wrong window."

So the continuity of life after death deals with what I call the starting point, training the eyes to see beyond appearances, to look out the right window, to see with a cosmic perspective. It means seeing concentrically, which means from within, seeing from the principle, seeing from God. But it is not seeing God, for no man has seen God at any time. It is looking out at life and seeing from the awareness of the allness of God. For God is not someone to see, but a perspective by which to see.

The poet Lowell describes this transcendental sense:

No man can think, nor in himself perceive,
Sometimes at waking, in the street sometimes,
Or on the hillside, always unforwarned,
A grace of being finer than himself,
That beckons and is gone,--a larger life
Upon his own impinging, with swift glimpse
Of spacious circles, luminous with mind,
To which the ethereal substance of his own
Seems but gross cloud to make that visible,
touched to a sudden glory round the edge.

In the book of Job, it says, "when they cast thee down, thou shall say, there is lifting up." If you can believe that something wonderful is going to happen to you, then you can accept it right now, then something wonderful has already happened, because you've touched a key level of consciousness. What it amounts to is not setting things right, but seeing them rightly. If you can decide that you're going to march to the beat of a different drummer, that you're going to seek to relate yourself to life and to people, to your work, and all conditions around you, to the highest level of consciousness and sing a new song, then you're going to experience a new insight in Truth and a new health or a division of health, love and loving relationships and

your hopes and aspirations will be visible on the tree of life.
  May the light dawn in your consciousness this day.

God bless you.
Ayin M. Adams, Msc.D., Ph.D.

Life Cannot Live
without Death
&
Death Cannot Live
Without Life

Section I

Life Cannot Live Without Death

The Eternal Secret of Life

"That, which the up reaching spirit can achieve,
The grand and all creative forces know,
They will assist and strengthen
As the light lifts up the acorn to the oak tree's height,
That is but to resolved and low,
God's whole great universe shall fortify thy soul."

- Eller Wheeler Wilcox

Suppose that with every setting sun,
there would follow no promise of a sunrise.
Suppose that with every falling of the leaves in November
there would be no resurgence of life in April.

Suppose that with every cut of the finger,
bruise of the knee, our life span was shortened.
Suppose that with every sorrow, discouragement
and despair, faith and hope would be lost, never to return.

The eternal secret of life, of healing, of celebration,
of overcoming, is only experienced on a cosmic level
and it is ours to experience only if we choose to march
to the beat of a different drummer
to view life from a different perspective.

There is a principle and a process that is repeatable.
The eternal secret: that regeneration and resurrection
is a part of life, there is no complete
understanding of life without them.

Nothing Echoes

Silence
dreaded Silence
dead Silence
there is no work,
there is no knowledge
there is no wisdom
in the grave

Sinew and flesh were upon
dry bones
black skin covered them
but there was no spirit in them

leaving the present state of the dead
without definition
separation
from the dream to the waking
from the waking to the dream
deep sleep has come.

Life after Death

My body sleeps for one night
one week, one month,
one year, or longer intervals
awaiting its slow awakening
to a new body.

Life- Death Cycles

He said that, "when you're dead
you're dead, and that's the end of you."

He believes that his knowledge
is within his brain and his brain is his mind
and that he has no connection with any other.

We are always eternal life
and within us are the life motions
and the repetitions of life-death cycles.

Prayer

Prayer
is
the contemplation
of the facts of life
from the highest point of view
lift up your eyes
lift up your awareness
become synchronized
feel It
resonate with It
this is prayer,
this is oneness
Prayer is the highest frequency of energy
Prayer is my experience
Prayer isn't something I force
Prayer isn't something I ask for
Prayer is my spiritual nature
Prayer is the very heart of my being.

Speak to Me

Winter of peace
seek me
prepare insidious joy
blood orange sunset
pregnant
slivering away
before the final darkness
radiant hues
speak to me.

Death Decaying

I too saw the raindrops fall from the trees
like morning dew on moist grass
like dry leaves, burnt brown
those winds were strong
they went raging around the house
sweeping the streets
emptying the people
silence
that went dead
what my ears heard
was a whispering
a mother crying
a mother whose earth lay weeping
seeping, mourning the death
of a forgotten lullaby
the memories gone
the grey ash
dead
I told my soul
that the sadness felt
was coming from my human self
again, I felt sadness
and told my soul
to burn a candle
in the chambers of the heart
and pray

Pray in
in the songs of change

Pray in
the winds of change

Pray in
the seasons of change

Pray in
for the fresh winds to blow

carving a niche
craving a hunger
of restoration
from the old meaning
of Life's Cycles
once again.

When At Last We Can No Longer Breathe

When at last we can no longer breathe
no longer breathe
smell our bodies burn
scorched, crisp, fried, died
and laid to the side
cold, frozen, stiff
we lay
on display
on a slab
in a silver metal drawer

no longer can we breathe
in that tangible air
or tell mother how much we love her
her strength, her vulnerability, her silence
and her son's death
no longer can we breathe

bodies laden
riddles with gun power
bullets ricochet and boomerang
making their exit
on black warm skin
red liquid oozes out
cold hard facts
spilt on streets
of death decaying
while cloudy tall mountains
loom against ominous dark skies
and I'll dream of you one last time
playing basketball on the court
of my heart
while dogs bark

at your insidious laughter
dragging your name through the rain...
oh black beauty
lift your powerful voice to the thunderous
applause of Oya
 sweet denizens of
Oshun
that we might meet
in higher realms
halls of justice
and know that
the brown strong boys
fall to the bullets of hate
in state, they lay on display
a small box
contains the remains
sustains
jewels for viewing
every sound in the stars
welcomes the hero home
listen to their drum beat
heart beat
to complete
a hero's return
from earth's density
propensity, scarcity
strive and the cycles of life
from the womb to the tomb
and back again.
When at last God whispers
I love you.

Belonging By Birth

We belong to the ocean
as if we belong to the rain
We belong to the morning
as if we belong to the night
we take flight
on wings, we sing
give rise to crackling voice
into the midnight sky
we live our choice
frolicking on the unsure shore line
where dark rainbows
play hide and seek
on Maui's sacred beach
we belong to the ocean
as if we belong to the rain
we belong to the morning
as if we belong to the night
we belong to death
and we belong by birth
and I cannot know
or pretend to know
where I will go
when I leave this world
perhaps into another
other world
for sure, I belong by birth.

Life Cannot Live Without Death & Death Cannot Live Without Life

Let us look together
and know, all that is left
is that you say YES to life
that you say YES to your good
that you say YES to that in you
which was discovered and demonstrated
by a Master teacher
over 2000 years ago
that calls us to remember
the great lesson
taught by Jesus
riding victoriously into Jerusalem
under that first Palm Sunday
whether it was a cross along the way
and a tomb
but believing implicitly
that the tomb was a tunnel
that had light at both ends
and the other end of the tunnel
was the light of Easter Sunday morning
was the light of the resurrection principle
was the light of life after death.
If you find yourself thinking
that life has handed you a cross,
it can lead you to an unexpected victory,
if you can get hold of it by the right end of it.

Section II

Death Cannot Live Without Life

A White Stone

You are the white of pureness,
the stone of stability, strength
and the identification.
You are part of a Divine plan
within you is the seed
 that longs to bear
its' perfect fruit
abundantly,
joyously.
and that
that is you cannot
be taken away
by anyone
It can never be severed
it can never be lost
it can never grow old.
It is always the eternal now
and it is always complete
in Spirit
with each word that you speak
with each idea
that you give birth to
with each unfoldment
that you are part of
you grow…
and you know more deeply
more profoundly than ever
your true identity, your Oneness
your wholeness.
You are
a seed
that is destined
to bring forth flowers

and at this moment
right where you are…
you are ready….
know yourself
respect your Divinity
accept your inheritance
make your commitment
and be joyous of the responsibility
that comes with spiritual fulfillment
that spark of you
that Divinity of you
which is created by the Infinite
and is
the Infinite
expressing
right where you are…
see it
and accept it.

Life after Death

Life after death
is a mystery
mankind's mystery
unexplored unknown
continuity finality
from the womb to the tomb
and back again
Oh noble death
you are here to take me
into my mystery, into my complete
conclusion, of my predestination
Oh noble death
this is a final farewell
falling away, absconding from this world
Oh noble death
I know that I am not the only one
for you will come to us all.

It is time to step off the eternal wheel of karma
and reincarnation Oh noble death
You have called to end my suffering and reemerge
into Oneness of life and death

Oh noble death
I placed an X above the door
in hopes of your passing
I think I hear your thumping
on the mud cracked house
oh noble death, is it the hour
have I completed the soul's sojourn on earth
is that why you knock, death?
listen if you will
to these three experiences

three trinities
hover no more beloved
do not fear
be not attached to this world
Oh Noble One
embrace the wholeness
of Life and Death
we release you to do so
I die to the past and am born
to the future

Restless Shadows

I am the canvas of eternity
my paintings have produced
every bit of success;
from the early murder
of my physical vessel
I never take anything personally
remain optimistic, creative
under stressful situations
poised and resilient throughout the death process
popping back up, becoming perceptive, intuitive
an emphatic leader
understanding the feelings of others
marks my success

I am a miracle worker
I have turned from the effects
of my restless shadows
Incubation
Syncopation
Reincarnation
Walk-in!

I am a canvas of eternity
my paintings have produced
healing and insight
joy and connection
on them
you see the intersection
of soul and thought
here and there
Brooklyn concrete and
cooled lava flow
of earth birthing in Hawaii

where I root and source

I am a miracle worker
I have turned from the effects
of my restless shadows
to the positive mind-set with the Infinite
and the inner knowing of my soul work
the resonance of my tuning
the depth of my growth
the incubation of my ever child
the syncopation of my beat
reincarnation of my life as a walk in.

The Gap

Between God's world and man's world
these two pulse
man's impulse: repulse.
life and death
are intervals
of rest
man detest
God express the best.
and when our loved ones die
emotions repressed
give rise from the oppress
to address
our grief and hidden anger no more
when we grieve
we perceived
from others, good deeds
is not in our best needs
I suggest the unrest
we must confess
without protest
or conquest
that the antidote for grief
to be cited
is knowledge
to be united
delighted and excited
in memories
of those we love.
when we know to the bone
that we cannot die or be alone
not even age or a crone
and that desire for body still
continue forever in the paternal,

maternal, external, fraternal,
infernal, nocturnal self eternal.
a new body will reappear
from that desire
just as surely as day follows night.
We will know Truth about
grief instead of misery
and welcome our mystery
with the synergy of our energy
and cast out hopelessness
due to ignorance.

Cease Clinging to Me

The teacher points to the truth
the student worships the pointer
therein lies the problem for much of
traditional Christianity, perhaps religion
of all kinds.
"Cease clinging to me."
Jesus said to Mary Magdalene
who was alone at the tomb
after the rest had gone
and Jesus came to her and said,
"Cease clinging to me."
Important words
that is often overlooked
in the life after death
resurrection story,
Cease clinging to me,
stop holding on to me"
and that's precisely
what we've done.
We've held on to Jesus
we've been holding on,
we've been looking to him
 worshipping the pointer
instead of the truth
that he pointed to.
He said,
"I must go away that I might come again."
I must get the physical personal self
out of the way, so that the radiant
Christ self can manifest.
The resurrection has everything
to do with Jesus, but it has had with most of us,
very little to do with us.

Alone

From the time I was born
I did not see
as others saw
I hid my passions
within the bright light of the sun
who exchange my sight
for a plight into the night
with my third eye
no pain, no gain, I could not cry,
to sustain the same
I could share and I could care
But I could not wake myself
From this nightmare
This realm, this plateau
which showed
me down deep
steep perhaps for keeps
into the underworld of walk-ins
and souls afore before taking form
Yet, my heart did beat
And I got to keep
Love that I could feel
pounding loud, sound
singing - songs of love
I claim my adult aloneness
like I claim my childhood
and I claim the warmth of
the fire crackling around me
heaven is near
I must take my rest
from the depth of life
into the regeneration pool
and I too, will love again eternally.

Who Is Responsible For You

Pay close attention to your thoughts.
you make your own misery
you make your own happiness

your thoughts are the only tools
with which you work
to remove the fools
that threaten to rule
your consciousness

play the leading actor
in your script

those who fail
have followed the laws of failure
those who succeed
have followed the laws of success

Truth never becomes our own
until we apply it
Truth never changes
but our understanding of it does

your today
is the result of your past thinking

one day your outer world will reveal
your inner thought-life and mimic it

I know what I am talking about
I once changed my mind
and within found the only place for which
results flow

I never again said a thing
that I did not want
to see realized in my life.
Whatever you put in
it's what emerges
choice
will affect your life
nothing nothing
nothing is ever forced upon you
without your consent
every moment of your waking life, you live,
you are choosing something every moment;
even now, in this poem you choose
to live, to die, to breathe, to hide, to run, to stop,
to find, to claim, to try, to cry, or even
to question or wonder why
what must always precede
the outer experience:
is an inner change
learn to use what you have been given
pay close attention to your thoughts.

Even After Death

I am grateful
for my life
and then it is no more
I am content
with nothing
but my existence
and then I am gone.

Even after death
I will love myself
even after death

when my time comes
I will meet myself
face to face
look lovingly into
beautiful brown eyes
welcome myself
back from the heavy dense
fog of human life

even after death
I will say
come let us meditate together
through winter's stillness
love will find its way back
to my heart and I shall know
that even after death
you have always loved me
although in my life
I have failed to listen to you
my heart, who have known
by heart, for all of my life

and through meditation
I shall return again and again and again
to love
even after death.

Hellos and Goodbyes

Life and death of bodies
are but thoughts that come and go
there are always
hellos and Goodbyes
in our calling

life and death record
their comings and goings
grow
flow
decay,
generate
radiate

there are always
hellos and Goodbyes
in our calling
my body
appear
disappear
reappear forever
bodies are wave cycles
of motion

death is a part of that motion
the notion of death and life
coming together in total rest
I address as always
evolving.

Mystery

They said to me,
"Who are you?
Why are you here?
What is your name."?

I said,
"On the day that you ask me
what is my mystery?
our relationship will begin."

Life is Temporal

We are born
we live
we die
many live as if
they do not know this.
Life is temporal.

Section III

The Continuity of Life

Dear Mother,

I want you to know that I see your grief and pain. I use to know pain and was very angry that my life was taken. He had no right to take my life. But now Mother, I am not concerned with setting things right, my focus is on seeing things rightly. I am now able to see from a higher awareness and with clarity. It was heavy for me on the planet to be weighed down with such heaviness as vengeance, violence, darkness, and grief. There is so much murkiness and denseness on earth.

All the experiences that are occurring on earth is occurring in man's reality, man's world, man's laws, man's punishments, man's justices, and has very little to do with love Mother. There is a spiritual law, which is unseen. Man has failed to utilize this gift. These laws set in motion Divine right action and work without seeing color, race, or creed. It is impermanent to those who use it.

I write this letter that bypasses your human senses, reaching deeply in your soul, to tell you that I understand forgiveness clearly. I know love Mother. You may call upon me for help, protection, and support. In my light of understanding and peace, forgiveness and oneness, I represent a wellspring from which you can lovingly draw strength and wisdom in times of need on the earth plane. It comes from Oneness.

I understand that you and countless other mothers are experiencing what may seem to be a lifetime of injustices and tribulations. Please know that these too, are a part of human existence. Do not become distracted by the loud noise that echoes around you. I ask you to go within. I urge you to ground yourself in love and forgiveness, using wisdom and understanding. I will help you with your fears and feelings of helplessness and insecurities, worries and anxieties.

I see the people on earth in grief, pain, and their temptations for violence and revenge. I see their unwavering marches and cries of more marches and rallies. I see no one comforting the people. Please know that I bring you comfort. Feel my presence mother, and know that I am with you always. Feel me breathe a cool peace upon your soul. You will come to know that together we will fulfill what needs to be done, for we have always been endowed from the beginning of mankind. We are resilient and extremely well fitted and equipped. Mother, when you choose to know, you will remember how we are connected to a greater power, stronger than any man of color, more prosperous than earthly finances and possessions. We are of a rare purity that is often punished, frowned upon, and inhumanly seized upon in a negative degrading way. All will be revealed in due time.

I want you to know that my entire journey on earth was monitored, because I needed to do my best, and I have completed my journey.

Mother, I speak directly to you in your dreams, in your prayers, and in the face of other men. Please know that we have made contact. Realize that deep down in your soul, we have reached one another.

I want to thank you for giving me the gift of life. I honor your life as mother, as a black woman, and as a feeling thinking praying woman. Thank you for being part of the sacred web of life. Now that you know these truths, you must go forth in love and compassion as you continue to evolve as a spiritual being, and growing through the human experience.

Know that I love you always Mother and that I forgive everyone and I ask you to forgive them too, for they know not what they do. I am free. I love you.

Until Soon,
Your Daughters and Sons,
Rekia Boyd, Aiyanna Jones, Miriam Carey, Yvette Smith, Tarika Wilson, Shantel Davis, Tyisha Miller, Gabriella Nevarez, Kathryn Johnston, Pearlie Golden, Sean Bell, Amadou Diallo, Cameron Tillman, VonDerrit Myers Jr., Rumain Brisbon, Akai Gurley, Rodney King, Trayvon Martin, Michael Brown, Eric Garner, Tamir Rice, Kajieme Powell, Ezell Ford, Dante Parker, Tyree Woodson, Victor White III, Yvette Smith, Jordan Baker, Jonathan Ferrell, Carlos Alcis, Larry Eugene Jackson, Jr., Deion Fludd, Kimani Gray, Chavis Carter, Tamon Robinson, Wendell Allen, Nehemiah Dillard, Manuel Loggins, Jr., Ramarley Graham, and others whose seat that we keep warm and their light which burns bright, make their way home.

Only birth can conquer death, the birth not of the old- thing again, but of something new. Peace is a snare, war is a snare, change is a snare, permanence a snare. When our days come for the victory of death- death closes in. There's nothing we can do, except be crucified and resurrected, dismembered totally, and then reborn.

Joseph Campbell, *A Hero with A Thousand Faces*

Spiritual Mind Treatments

What is Spiritual Mind Treatment: Treatment is the act, the art and the science of inducing thought within the mentality of the one treating, which thought shall perceive that the body of the patient is a Divine, Spiritual and Perfect Idea.

Dr. Ernest Holmes

The One Eternal Principle of life is all there is. There is God and there is nothing else—God, The Good, and Omnipotent. It is Absolute Good, Absolute Harmony, Absolute Beauty, Absolute Joy and this Great One celebrates life by means of me. I am a center of Divine Love from which all originates. In this recognition of my Divine Self, I realize that there is nothing to fear. In this spiritual awareness, I am empowered in consciousness to recognize this truth. The Divine Nature surrounds me, enfolds me and supports me moment by moment. I can never escape the Divine Embrace. I express the love of God and it returns to me as a joyous action in my world and I give thanks and so it is.

In this moment of recognizing and realizing, I accept the Presence of God operating in me and everywhere. The Presence that is the perfect expression of love, wisdom, beauty and abundance is the Divine Presence within me enjoying the One Life that is my life. There is One Life, and that Life is God, the Life of Infinite Mind, and I am that Life. I do not own life. Life owns me and uses me as Its self-expression. This Life is pure Intelligence. This Life is absolute and total love. God's Life is indestructible, and I am this Life in action. I always have been, I am now and evermore shall be. I am eternal. I am the unlimited expression of that Life which is unlimited, unconditioned and free. I am never conclusion; I am always possibility. I am cause to my world of effects and I make certain to create only the good. I cannot defeat myself, no matter what methods and means I may select. Mind in me remains untouched by my experience and directs me to right answers. I am inwardly motivated to create and fulfill abundant life. I do this for myself, thus fulfilling the Spirit which I am.

As I celebrate this season of peace, love, and joy, I recognize the Infinite and eternal Love of God is forever expressing through me. I gladly share this gift of Love with all those in my life, knowing that what I send out must always return to me many times multiplied. I celebrate the One Life, the One Power and Presence that is operating by means of me. In this realization I am empowered in consciousness to use this creative power for my greater good. As I declare this greater good it moves into my life and I become a channel of blessings for the Divine to express. I give thanks knowing that the One Infinite Mind is inspiring me to greater heights of spiritual awareness. And so it is.

There is One Creative Action in the universe. It is in an eternal process of giving and creating out of Itself. It is God, Infinite Mind, Source, Oneness, and Universal Creative Intelligence. It is the Great Prospering Principle awaiting expression by means of me. It is the single Source of all that is. It is the very Principle of Life made manifest. This One Source is the Source of all that I am right now. It is the Source of all that I will ever be. I accept this Divine Flow of good operating through me and prospering me right now. I open my heart to receive and appreciate the opulent givingness of Spirit. I release anything and everything that would block this abundant demonstration of the bounty of God's perfect love.

There is One Power, One Creative Intelligence, One Mind, One Infinite and Eternal Source called God, the good, omnipotent, omnipresence, and omniscience. This Power expresses as Life, the One Life, the Life of God expressing through me. That Life is perfect, whole and complete. It is peace love and joy. The One Mind that is the Creative Action of Life is individualized and operating by means of me. That One Mind is operating within the leaders of all nations and bringing about guidance to reveal the avenue to the right resolution of conflicts facing our world. Everything necessary for the fulfillment of this Perfect Action already exists in the universe and within all. I accept that this Perfect Action is taking place right now for my greater good and the good of all mankind. And so it is.

My demonstration of Life is the Creative Action of the Divine operating by means of my consciousness. Therefore, right now my greater acceptance and embodiment of the Divine expressing by means of me empowers and expands my consciousness. As Spirit-in-action, I am unburdened of all worry, doubts and fear and I celebrate the gift of Life expressing as me. Knowing that all things are possible, I move from good to greater good in this perfect expression of the Divine. And so it is.

There is a Power and Presence for good operating in my life right now. I declare my independence from the world of effect operating around me. I recognized my total dependence upon Spirit to create my greater expression of life. In this great realization everything in my experience moves in Divine Synchronicity. The right people, at the right time, at the right place and under the right circumstance, cooperate to manifest my prospering and joyous demonstration of good. Nothing in me obstructs my acceptance of the Divine gifts flowing into m life. I allow myself the freedom to express that One Life in ever expanding avenues of love. And so it is.

I am a center of Divine Operation. The One Infinite Mind and the One Power and Presence are always operating by means of me. This Divine Presence creates everything and is creating a new beginning in my life right now. I recognize that this day and every day presents me with a fresh opportunity to begin anew. Since God is at the center of all that I am and all that I do, I celebrate my life and live without fear or worry. This indwelling Power and Presence is an Infinite Potential awaiting expression by means of me, therefore, I make the right decisions at the right time for Divine Right Action. I am always supported and sustained by this Presence in every endeavor in life.

Today I celebrate this day in joyful thanksgiving as I await my greater demonstration of good. And so it is.

Steps for Giving a Spiritual Mind Treatment

Before beginning our treatment, we must first decide what we will be treating for, in other words what is our goal. We must be very clear in our thinking as to what we will treat for to move it into our lives. If we are not clear and specific, then our demonstration will reflect in that same way. We only attract what we understand.

We will need to state in the beginning of our treatment for whom we are treating. "This word is spoken for me, (give your name)" or this treatment is spoken for "Mary Jones" or whomever.

Step One Identification - Recognizing our Source of Good

We identify our Divine Source. "There is One God, One Divine Power, One Creative Action in the Universe, One Universal Spirit."

Step Two Unification - Uniting ourselves with our Divine Source

Recognize that we are part of God and not separate from that Divine Power and Presence. We are creations of God and we are expressing God. We identify ourselves with God by a conscious, intelligent sensing and feeling of the Divine Presence within. All that God is, we are. "I am the individualized expression of God."

Step Three - Declaration of Purpose

We express the good we desire as a "Spiritual Idea." We must establish in our thought a complete idea: definite, clear and specific. Our declaration must be an emphatic statement of only what we want. Our words must be spoken with authority and conviction. Our words are directed into the Mind of God resident within us. Our statements are made "in the now." We are living in the now and our demonstration of good must be made in the now.

Since the Mind of God knows only that which is perfect, whole and complete, we must state our desire as a "spiritual idea". We must totally accept this idea as manifesting in our lives as we speak our word in treatment.

Step Four - Denials and Affirmations

We make very brief statements of the denials of any fear, loss, lack or limitation operating within our conscious or subconscious mind. We quickly make this denial and release any blockages that would prevent our full acceptance of our good.

Step Five - Affirming and Accepting Our Good

We must affirm and accept our good. The word we have spoken in treatment is appearing and manifesting in our life right now. We accept that our good, that which we desire is an accomplished fact; we affirm the good, the true and the beautiful taking place in our lives.

Step Six - Releasing Our Word

We release our word to the Law of Mind and the Law of Mind does the work. We release our word knowing it moves in Divine Action to manifest in our lives. "These words that I have spoken are now acted upon by the Law of Cause and Effect. It is done. And so it is."

When we have cut ourselves off from the true branch
The negation of not seeing the true source of life
Rain comes down as a physical dissolution of the body
A parting of ways, a long sleep into death
as the soul enters into a deep silence."

Scriptural Readings

John 1:12

But to all who have received him–those who believe in his name–he has given the right to become God's children.

John 3:16

For God so loved the world that He gave His one and only Son, that everyone who believes in Him shall not perish but have eternal life.

John 5:13

I have written these things to you who believe in the name of the Son of God; so that you may know that you have eternal life.

John 5:24-25

I tell you the solemn truth, the one who hears my message and believes the one who sent me has eternal life and will not be condemned, but has crossed over from death to life. I tell you the solemn truth, a time is coming–and is now here–when the dead will hear the voice of the Son of God, and those who hear will live.

John 6:47-50

"I tell you the truth; anyone who believes has eternal life. Yes, I am the bread of life! Your ancestors ate manna in the wilderness, but they all died. Anyone who eats the bread from heaven, however, will never die."

John 11:11

These things said he: and after that he saith unto them, our friend Lazarus sleepeth; but I go, that I may awake him out of sleep.

John 11: 23-25

Jesus saith unto her, "Thy brother shall rise again. Martha saith unto him, I know that he shall rise again in the resurrection at the last day. Jesus said unto her, I am the resurrection, and the life: he that believeth in me, though he was dead, yet shall he live."

John 14:1-3

Let not your heart be troubled: ye believe in God, believe also in me.
In my Father's house are many mansions: if it were not so, I would have told you. I go to prepare a place for you. And if I go and prepare a place for you, I will come again, and receive you unto myself; that where I am, there ye may be also.

John 14: 10-14

Believest thou not that I am in the Father, and the Father in me? The words that I speak unto you I speak not of myself: but the Father that dwelleth in me, he doeth the works.
Believe me that I am in the Father, and the Father in me: or else believe me for the very works' sake. Verily, verily, I say unto you, He that believeth on me, the works that I do shall he do also; and greater works than these shall he do; because I go unto my Father. And whatsoever ye shall ask in my name, that will I do, that the Father may be glorified in the Son. If ye shall ask any thing in my name, I will do it.

John 17: 1-3

These words spake Jesus, and lifted up his eyes to heaven, and said, Father, the hour is come; glorify thy Son, that thy Son also may glorify thee: As thou hast given him power over all flesh, that he should give eternal life to as many as thou hast given him. And this is life eternal, that they might know thee the only true God, and Jesus Christ, whom thou hast sent.

Hebrews 9:27

...and just as it is appointed for people to die...and after this, judgment.

Matthew 25:46

These people will go away...but the righteous will go into eternal life.

Romans 6:23

For the wages of sin is death; but the gift of God is eternal life through Jesus Christ our Lord.

1 Corinthians 2:9

But as it is written, Eye hath not seen, nor ear heard, neither have entered into the heart of man, the things which God hath prepared for them that love him.

Luke 23:43, 46

And Jesus said unto him, Verily I say unto thee, today shalt thou be with me in paradise.
And when Jesus had cried with a loud voice, he said, Father, into thy hands I commend my spirit: and having said thus, he gave up the ghost.

Hebrews 13:14

For here have we no continuing city, but we seek one to come.

Revelation 21:4

And God shall wipe away all tears from their eyes; and there shall be no more death, neither sorrow, nor crying, neither shall there be any more pain: for the former things are passed away.

Romans 8:6

For to be carnally minded is death; but to be spiritually minded is life and peace.

2 Corinthians 4:16

For which cause we faint not; but though our outward man perish, yet the inward man is renewed

1 Timothy 4:8

For bodily exercise profited little: but godliness is profitable unto all things, having promise of the life that now is, and of that which is to come.

Ecclesiastics 12: 5-7

Also when they shall be afraid of that which is high, and fears shall be in the way, and the almond tree shall flourish, and the grasshopper shall be a burden, and desire shall fail: because man goeth to his long home, and the mourners go about the streets: Or ever the silver cord be loosed, or the golden bowl be broken, or the pitcher be broken at the fountain, or the wheel broken at the cistern. Then shall the dust return to the earth as it was: and the spirit shall return unto God who gave it.

Revelation 14:11

And the smoke of their torment ascendeth up forever and ever: and they have no rest day or night, who worships the beast and his image, and whosoever receiveth the mark of his name.

Revelation 21:8

But the fearful, and unbelieving, and the abominable, and murderers, and whoremongers, and sorcerers, and idolaters, and all liars, shall have their part in the lake which burneth with fire and brimstone: which is the second death.

The Will of God

God cannot be life enriching and death producing at the same time.

God's will is the ceaseless longing of the Creator, to perfect himself in all he creates. And this longing can be channeled into an irresistible force for health, for wise guidance, for ample and continuous supply. Sickness often comes from a will to be sick and that health if truly sought, must be preceded by a will to be well, the will to live, the will to overcome, the will to rise above the difficulty.

I will to be well, gather the forces of mind and body about the central idea of wholeness, and the will holds the center as long as the I AM continues its affirmation. It's an interesting thought, "I will to be well." I will to overcome. I will to achieve. We can live as long as we really want to live, if we set our goals and work towards the fulfillment of them.

It could be said that no one ever really dies, until he gives up the Will to live. And we doubt this, through the deterioration of morale, and the physical pain and so forth, that there comes a lessening of the will, but as long as a person, really wills to be well and wills to go on, he will overcome, and he will go on.

Let's set our goals and work towards the fulfillment of them, work at living, there will be no fear of dying.

Imaging Exercise: Prayer

You are going to experience a different kind of prayer, perhaps it isn't a prayer, and perhaps it is more a movement of consciousness which could be what prayer really is anyway.
We're going to have an imaging exercise. I want you to think for a moment of a tree, just imagine a tree, any kind of a tree. Genesis talks about the tree of life, which refers to a living process, in which we all live, move, and have our being. Get a picture of that tree in consciousness, maybe a tree in your yard at home, a tree that you've seen in the park, a beautiful tree, see it full of leaves, let that tree be to you, a source of one of the branches which we'll isolate as a positive healing bow on the tree.
Look carefully at that healing bow, let it be to you, your aspirations, your dream of change and overcoming, your desire to be what you like to be, your inner urge, your inclinations to prosper, to succeed, to be affluent, to be healed, to experience love, to be loved.
Believe for a moment that which the ancient ones believed; that if the positivity is held in your mind, there will come one day to stay a singing bird. It will manifest in your life. This is your image; you can do anything you want with it.
It does not matter what kind of bird it is, or the color, or the size, or the song the bird sings. See that bird on the positive healing branch, feel it, experience it in your chambers of imagery a singing bird on that positive branch as it sings heartily of its song. See it as the symbol of your healing, in that moment something wonderful has happened to you, you'll never be the same again. The stone of limitation has been rolled away, keep the covenant suggested by the ancient ones, keep the positive branch in your mind, there will come one day and to stay, a singing bird.
When you finish this book, or complete this exercise, I want you to take with you this image, perhaps take time before the day is over, in the quiet of your home or in the park, reproduce this image, a tree, its positive healing branch and a singing bird. Remember

it represents your aspirations, your hopes, your ideals, your objectives, your goals, represents your fulfillment, the answer to your every need, fulfillment of your prayers.
Join with me in consciousness and excitement about this idea, carry with you a sense of rejoicing throughout this day which shall be for you a new day of the continuity of life and realizing that life cannot live without death and death cannot live without life. As Jesus said, you shall know the truth and the truth shall make you free. So be it. And so it is.

About the Author

Ayin M. Adams, Msc.D., PhD., is a native New Yorker. She is also an international metaphysician, spiritual director, and intuitive therapist. Adams is a holistic teacher of self-development and consciousness. Adams utilizes her gift of words to heal, educate, and entertain.

Adams is the author of more than eight books. Adams has been published by "Women in the Moon" publishing, *Bum Rush The Page*, *In The Family*, and *Quiet Mountain Essays*. Adams is the 2015 Beverly Hills Book Awards Finalist for her book, *African Americans in Hawai`i: A Search for Identity*, the 2015 *Bronze Medal Illumination Book Award* winner, 1998 winner of the *Pat Parker Poetry Award*, the 1999 *Audre Lorde Memorial Prose Prize*, the 2001 *President's Award for Literary Excellence*, and the *Zora Neal Hurston/Richard Wright Award*. Adams documents our passage in time using her writings and tonality of voice to help one break out of the current constraints and fragmentation of daily and habitual life. She assists

and facilitates individuals to co-create their futures, especially as many of the established structures of society may be falling apart. Adams lives with the intention of suiting up, showing up, and following through. Adams embraces a firm belief that everything is in Divine Order. Ayin M. Adams organizes and leads spiritual retreats geared towards the transformational transcendence of mind, body, and soul. She makes her home in Maui. You may visit her at www.ayinadams.com.

www.ingramcontent.com/pod-product-compliance
Lightning Source LLC
Chambersburg PA
CBHW060503110426
42738CB00055B/2610